The Rockwool Foundation Research Unit

Does Incarceration Length Affect Labor Market Outcomes for Violent Offenders?

Rasmus Landersø

University Press of Southern Denmark
Odense 2012

Does Incarceration Length Affect Labor Market Outcomes for Violent Offenders?

Study Paper No. 39

Published by:
© The Rockwool Foundation Research Unit and University Press of Southern Denmark

Copying from this book is permitted only within institutions that have agreements with CopyDan, and only in accordance with the limitations laid down in the agreement

Address:
The Rockwool Foundation Research Unit
Sølvgade 10
DK-1307 Copenhagen K

Telephone   +45 33 34 48 00

Fax   +45 33 34 48 99

E-mail   forskningsenheden@rff.dk

Home page   www.rff.dk

ISBN 978-87-90199-65-4
ISSN 0908-3979
January 2012
Print run: 350
Printed by   Specialtrykkeriet Viborg A/S

Price: 60.00 DKK, including 25% VAT

Contents

Abstract   5

1 Introduction   6

2 Background   7

3 Data   11

4 Econometric Framework   17

5 Results   18

6 Conclusion   25

References   28

Does Incarceration Length Affect Labor Market Outcomes for Violent Offenders?

Rasmus Landersø,[*]

Rockwool Foundation Research Unit

Abstract This paper uses a reform of the Danish Penal Code concerning violent crimes to study the effects of an exogenous increase in incarceration length on labor market outcomes during the first three years after release, meassured by unemployment rates, dependency on other public transfers, and earnings. Using a panel of monthly observations constructed from detailed Danish administrative-level data, I track a sample of violent offenders from four years prior to incarceration to conclude that the reform provided an exogenous increase in incarceration length and that the outcomes for the two groups exibitibit equal trends. I find lower unemployment rates and a higher level of earnings for those employed as an effect of the longer incarceration spells induced by the reform. In addition, the effects of the reform increase with passage of time after release.

Keywords Crime, Incarceration length, Labor market outcomes.

Acknowledgements I am grateful for the advice and comments of the Danish Prison and Probation Service, Signe Hald Andersen, and Anne Marie Heckscher and Helle Risbjerg from Sønder Omme State Prison, as well as the participants at the Rockwool Foundation Research Unit's brown bag seminar and at the EALE conference 2011.

---

[*]Corresponding author. Rockwool Foundation Research Unit, Sølvgade 10, 2. tv, DK-1307 K Copenhagen. Web: www.rff.dk. Email: rl@rff.dk.

1 Introduction

The aim of this paper is to assess the causal effect of the length of an incarceration spell on subsequent unemployment rates, dependency on other public transfers, and earnings, for a sample of violent offenders. Earlier investigations in this field have been inconclusive, as they have struggled to handle the complex relationships between crime, labor market outcomes and unobserved characteristics while using samples which consist of different and heterogeneous offender types (e.g. Lott (1992a,b); Needles (1996); Kling (2006)). To estimate the causal effect of incarceration length on labor market outcomes, it is necessary to address the problem that individuals serving prison sentences of different lengths are likely to differ in terms of a number of observable and unobservable characteristics. For this purpose, I make use of a reform of the Danish Penal Code which increased incarceration lengths for violent offenders in a way that was unrelated to their individual behavioural characteristics, thus providing exogenous variation. I construct a detailed panel of monthly observations using Danish administrative-level data, and analyze the sample for a period from four years before incarceration until three years after release.

The previous literature on the field of sanctions for crime and subsequent labor market outcomes has mainly focussed on the effect of conviction or incarceration *per se*. However, once a person has been found guilty of a crime, policy-makers and judges not only face a discrete choices as to whether to punish the offender for the crime or not, or as to whether the sanction should be a prison sentence or not. They also face the important decision in determining the length of the incarceration spell if the offender is sentenced to imprisonment.

The chosen length of an incarceration spell may affect the offender's labor market productivity positively or negatively, depending on whether the offender loses or accumulates human capital while incarcerated. The incarceration length may also affect the offender's future life-course in other ways. Informal sanctions from society produced by stigma might influence job opportunities for former prison inmates and imply that complete redemption is never possible. In addition, informal sanctions associated with incarceration length may amplify the intended sentence. A longer incarceration spell may not necessarily result in worse labor market outcomes, as it might facilitate participation in various rehabilitation programmes and training. Such participation may increase human and social capital while strengthening personal traits, and may consequently result in a positive effect on subsequent labor market outcomes.

I find that the longer incarceration spells induced by the reform result in lower unemployment rates and higher levels of earnings for those who do obtain employment. These results suggest that sentences can be too short, as they may leave the offender stigmatized but with no chance of entering rehabilitation programmes, etc. Hence, an increase in incarceration length - as induced by the reform - improves labor market outcomes with the improvement in the conditions for rehabilitation.

The remainder of the paper is organized as follows: Section 2 provides the background of the paper by introducing the link between incarceration length and labor market outcomes. In addition, Section 2 briefly reviews the previous literature and findings in this field and highlights the problems faced by this paper and the proposed solutions to these. Section 3 introduces the data and provides descriptive statistics for the sample. Section 4 introduces the econometric framework and Section 5 presents the results of the estimations along with specification tests. Section 6 concludes.

2 Background

Theory suggests that productivity determines wage earnings y, and further that experience on the labor market and level of education determine productivity, as e.g. proposed in the seminal works by Becker (1994); Mincer (1974). Here I relax the original description of earnings, and let y denote any labor market outcome - including earnings, unemployment benefits, and reception of other public transfers. Also, many empirical studies show that the components of education and experience do not account for all differences between various individuals' labor market outcomes (see e.g. Jencks (1972); Cunha and Heckman (2008); Cunha, Heckman, and Schennach (2010)). The residual differences may arise due to differences in network-connections within the labor market (or alternatively in social capital,[1] see e.g. Granovetter (1995)) along with search behavior (see e.g. Holzer (1988)). I.e. the effort in job-search, the productivity of the search method along with general contacts and social bonds within the labor market are contributing factors to employment status and subsequent earnings. The central theme of this paper is how incarceration of length I affects the labor market outcome y, either directly or as a consequence of changes in e.g. human capital, search behaviour etc. While level of education and age often serve as proxies for human capital, actual human and social capital along with search behavior are - though affected by observable characteristics - largely unobserved. Thus may the channels through which incarceration can affect labor market outcomes be unobserved as well.

The effects of an incarceration spell consists in two elements. The first effect arises from the incarceration *per se*, and the second arises from the length of the incarceration spell.

I express the first effect, describing how incarceration *per se* affects an offender's future labor market outcomes, as $dy/dI\,|_{I=0}$. A vast literature investigates this (for notable examples see Freeman (1992); Waldfogel (1994); Nagin and Waldfogel (1995); Grogger (1995); Nagin and Waldfogel (1998); Western, Kling, and Weiman (2001)). Most of the studies find a negative association; that is $dy/dI\,|_{I=0} < 0$ (when considering outcomes such as earnings or employment and the opposite when considering outcomes such as unemployment). The literature generally ascribes this finding to stigma from the incarceration, as employers who face imperfect information may use criminal records as signals, revealing otherwise unobserved characteristics.

The second effect - the effect of the incarceration length once sentenced to imprisonment, and thus the effect in focus in this paper - is captured by $dy/dI\,|_{I>0}$. The sign of this is ambiguous, as incarceration length may affect the subsequent labor market outcomes in different ways. On one hand, a longer incarceration spell may result in depreciation of human capital as offenders lose skills and productivity in general or miss potential work-experience and consequently, do not face the same productivity growth as non-incarcerated workers (see e.g. Waldfogel (1994); Western, Kling, and Weiman (2001)). Longer incarceration spells may also depreciate social capital by eroding personal connections which match workers to employers or provide information about possible job opportunities (see e.g. Sampson and Laub (1995)). On the other hand, longer incarceration spells may increase offenders' productivity, e.g. through an increased likelihood of enterring treatment for substance abuse

---

[1] The economic literature on social capital is much sparser than that on human capital. For an introduction e.g. see Glaeser, Laibson, and Sacerdote (2002). A related concept that has received much attention in recent years is that of *non-cognitive skills*. For a review of the relevant literature e.g. see Almlund, Duckworth, Heckman, and Kautz (2011).

or through education or training while incarcerated (see e.g. Kling (2006)). Further, longer incarceration spells may facilitate participation in rehabilitating programs or assistance in job search, thus lowering the costs of finding a job or increasing social capital, ceteris paribus (a proposition put forward as early as the mid-19th century by criminologist Arnould Bonneville De Marsangy). Which effects and theoretical concepts that dominate depends on the nature of the incarceration. If the incarceration spell is long it may affect level of human capital and thus earnings or employment status significantly, whether in a positive or a negative direction. However, I propose that only incarceration spells of a certain length can cause such a change in level of human capital. Hence, for short incarceration spells, changes in contacts within the labor market or stigma may be the dominant forces.

While there is a substantial literature investigating the first effect, the literature on the second effect of incarceration length on labor market outcomes is much sparser. Furthermore, the results from the literature that does exist are inconclusive. Lott (1992a) estimates a first-difference model on a sample of convicted drug-offenders and finds no significant association between sentencing length and the difference in earnings before and after prison. In contrast, Lott (1992b) (again estimating a first-difference model) finds a significant monetary penalty to offenders convicted of larceny or theft. The estimates show that serving one additional month in prison reduces post-release earnings by as much as 32 percent compared to pre-incarceration earnings. In contrast, Lott's estimated effects to offenders convicted of embezzlement- or fraud were insignificant. Needles (1996) uses a quasi-experiment of randomly assigned "Transitional Aids"[2] to newly-released prisoners convicted of various types of crime. When examining the marginal changes in incarceration length by using a two-step Heckman procedure, to control for selection into employment, she finds no significant effect on earnings. Kling (2006) uses an instrumental variable of randomly-assigned judges as exogenous variation in time incarcerated on a sample of various types of offenders convicted by the federal judicial system in California.[3] He finds no significant effects from incarceration length on either future employment or earnings nine years after the beginning of the incarceration spell. The study further finds relatively small positive but significant short-term effects from incarceration length on future employment and earnings (one and two-and-a-half years after release respectively), using data from the Florida state prison system together with the Californian sample (Kling does, however, stress that lack of exogenous variation in the latter model may bias the estimates). In addition, Kling suggests that the results arise because longer incarceration spells might enhance the possibility of receiving assistance that increases employability once released, such as treatment for substance abuse. Finally, Tranæs (2008); Landersø and Tranæs (2009), using a sample including incarcerated property and violent offenders in Denmark, identify a fall in wages and labor market attachment together with an increase in dependency on public transfers from before to after incarceration. However, their conclusions ignore possible biases caused by unobserved individual characteristics and the possibly endogenous relationship between incarceration length and labor market outcomes.

These opposing results from previous studies underline the ambiguity mentioned earlier, and hence $dy/dI\,|_{I>0}$ is unknown. This is a point that emphasizes the complexity of the research question posed here. Different incarceration lengths may correlate with unobserved individual characteristics that also affect labor market outcomes. Incarceration length is then

---

[2] A programme designed to help newly-released prisoners rehabilitate, see Needles (1996).
[3] Inmates of federal prisons must have committed a crime defined as "being within federal jurisdiction". Kling mentions "interstate postal fraud and some drug cases" as examples of such crimes.

endogenous to labor market outcomes, which obscures the results and the causal reading of the estimates. Some of the existing studies use first difference or fixed effects estimations to obviate time-invariant unobserved individual characteristics that affect both employability and proneness to crime. However, these frameworks do not eliminate any probable relationships between unobserved time-varying components and labor market conditions; for example if layoffs, paycuts, etc. prior to the incarceration spark crime. In such cases, previous levels of labor market outcomes or shocks will correlate with the length of the subsequent incarceration spell, which means that simply eliminating the individual fixed effects is insufficient. One solution to this problem of endogeneity is to implement an instrumental variable, as Kling (2006) does. However, his study suffers from an analogous problem of heterogeneous sample composition, since he uses a sample of pooled offender types, as other previous studies do.

Assuming homogeneous treatment effects in the samples of pooled, but fundamentally different offender types, may bias conclusions in arbitrary directions. This paper proposes a setup that will take these problems into account, by applying a reform of the Danish Penal Code in 2002 that allows me to identify the effect of incarceration length on subsequent labor market outcomes. The reform only affected a specific group of offenders, namely those convicted of a specific type of violent crime. In addition, the reform was unrelated to any fixed or varying behavioural characteristics of the offenders, as it applied generally.

2.1 The Reform of the Penal Code

On the 31st of May 2002 the Danish government made a change to the Penal Code concerning violent crime. The change raised the maximum sentence length for "simple violence"[4] from 1 year and 6 months to 3 years. The bill was immediately put into effect, and has thus affected all sanctions for violent crimes committed after the 31st of May 2002. The aim of the bill was explained as follows:

The government finds that the previous level of sanctions in cases of crime harming others does not adequately reflect the victims' suffering. Hence, the government wishes to increase the sanctions for such crimes. [Justification for the bill by Secretary of Justice Lene Espersen (2002), own translation]

Thus, the reform targeted violent offenders in general and increased the sanctions for a given violent crime.

Figure 1 shows the monthly average lengths of incarceration for the sample[5] investigated in this paper.

---

[4]For a legal definition of the term see https://www.retsinformation.dk/Forms/R0710.aspx?id=126465.
[5]I will introduce the sample formally in Section 3.

Figure 1: Monthly averages of incarceration lengths

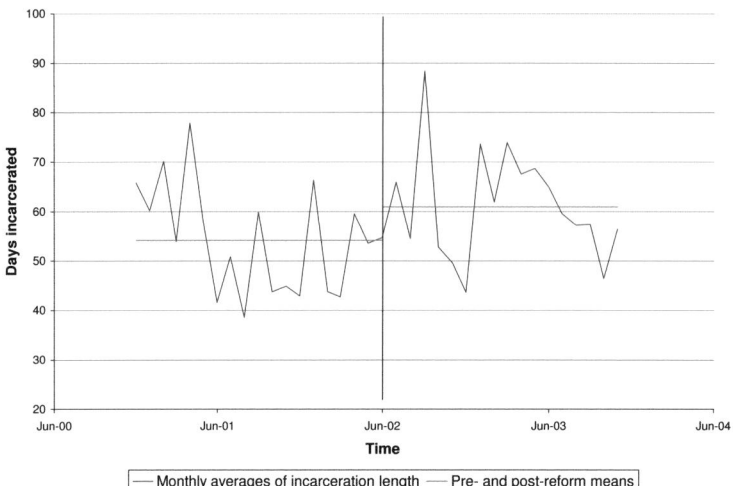

Source: Based on own calculations using data from Statistics Denmark.

The figure shows that the average incarceration length was far below the maximum sentence length both before and after the reform. Nevertheless, the average incarceration length increased from 54.13 days before the reform to 60.96 days after it, an increase of 12.6 percent.[6] Further, the median incarceration lengths across the reform increased from 38 to 44 days.

The justification shows that the reform was meant to have a homogeneous effect, by targeting both first-time offenders and those with long criminal records. However, it is unclear whether the reform, for example, only affected the sentence lengths of the few individuals who committed the most serious offences of (simple) violence (the ones whose sentences were bounded by the maximum sentence length) or the lengths of all sentences. Figure 2 shows the distributions of incarceration lengths in the sample for individuals committing crime prior to and after the reform respectively.[7]

Both distributions are heavily concentrated in the interval 20 to 70 days, with peaks at 30 and 60 days which correspond to sentences of one and two months of imprisonment respectively. However, as is evident from the figure, it seems that the entire distribution shifts to the right after the reform, as the post-reform distribution in general shows fewer sentences in the interval in the lower part of the sentence range and a larger number of sentences at the high end of the range. There do not seem to be remarkable differences between the tails of the two distributions which might question whether the reform increased the incarceration length for all offenders. However, as a consequence of the few observations receiving sentences above 70 days any non-extreme changes would be undetectable in practice. I therefore conclude, in the light of figure 2 and the rationale of the bill, that the incarceration length to any type of violent crime within the category of simple violence was increased by the reform.

---

[6]The change is significant with a p-value < 0.01.

[7]The figure has been censored at 150 days. The censored data corresponds to 5.26 percent of the sample prior to the reform and 6.30 after it.

Data

Figure 2: Pre- and post-reform distributions of incarceration length

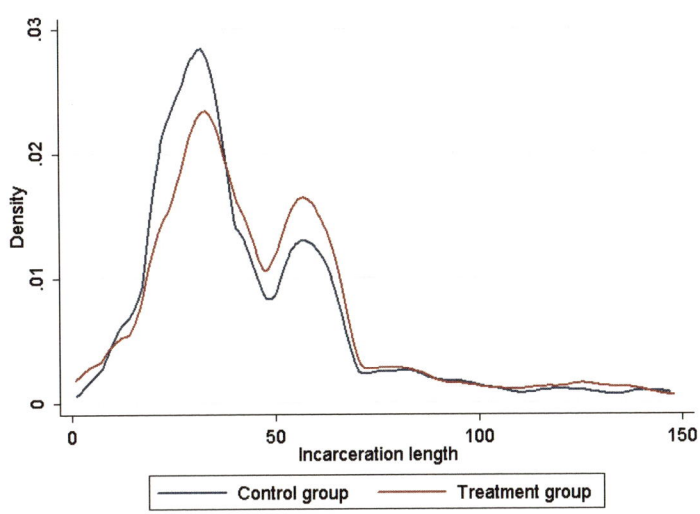

Source: Based on own calculations using data from Statistics Denmark.

However, as figure 2 shows, much of the increase in average length arose because of increases in incarceration length from one to two months, for a proportion of the sample.

Regardless of the exact effect of reform on incarceration lengths, Danish prisons provide offenders, who serve less than three months with few or no opportunities to participate in programmes or receive treatment with rehabilitating focus. The underlying reason is practical, as these short spells og imprisonment provide insufficient time for caseworkers to be assigned, courses to start, and general plans to be drafted for implementation at the time of release.

3 Data

The paper uses administrative data from Statistics Denmark[8] on criminal records, education, earnings, age, gender, ethnicity, marital status and children, along with information on recipients of public transfers from the DREAM database.[9] The various information is linked by an individual-specific social security number. Further, the criminal registers include a unique case-specific code, verdict (guilty, acquitted), sentence type (imprisonment, suspended sentence, fine, warning, detainment), date of crime, type of crime, incarceration date, release date, type of incarceration (e.g. remand, serving term of imprisonment, etc.). I only consider an individual criminal if she has been convicted of a crime and no subsequent

---

[8] Only Danish residents are included in the registers.

[9] Contains information on every Danish citizen who has received public benefits/transfers of any kind. For further information see: http://www.dst.dk/upload/microsoft_word_-_beskrivelse_af_dream_koder_-___version_22.pdf.

appeals are in process. I further discard all types of convictions that did not result in an sentence of imprisonment[10] for simple violence from the data.

The frequency of violent crime decreases with age and the majority of crimes are committed by men. As a consequence I censor the data to only include men who were aged 45 or younger at the date of the crime,[11] in order to ensure homogeneity between the individuals in the sample. Further, as special conditions apply for individuals below the age of 18, I only include adults of 18 or above.

The data are available for several years prior to and after incarceration. Hence, I create a panel with one time series per individual per case (which led to a conviction to imprisonment for simple violence). Since individuals in the sample served their specific prison sentence at different points in time, I create a seperate time-line. I denote month at the start of incaceration as time 0, the month prior to this time -1, and so forth. Similarly, I denote the first month after release time 1, the subsequent month time 2, and so forth, and delete all points in time from the incarceration date to the release date, for all individuals.

The analysis only includes observations related to crimes committed between December 2000 and November 2003. The sample thus consist of individuals incarcerated as a consequence of simple violence committed within a period of 18 months on each side of the reform. I have chosen this time-span to reach a sample size that on one hand obviates random variation, and on the other does not allow changing demographics and macro-trends to compromise the comparability between the earlier and later parts of the sample. The group that committed crime before the reform is the control group, and the group that committed crime after the reform is the treatment group. No individual in the sample experienced more than one incarceration for simple violence during the time-span considered in this paper.

For estimation purposes, I discard the individuals who experienced incarceration prior to the specific incarceration at time 0 and were not released at least 12 months before. Additionally, some individuals experienced further incarceration, emigrated or died during the three years after release. In order to avoid multiple treatments and attrition, I discard these from the sample. The panel is thus perfectly balanced. This censoring applies to 43 and 40 persons from the treatment and control groups respectively (2.5 and 2.2 percent of the final sample). Of these, a sizeable proportion are excluded due to death or emigration after release. Only 48 persons in total (22 from the control group and 26 from the treatment group) are discarded from the sample as a result of a sentence of imprisonment, a suspended sentence or unexplained events during the first three years after release. The censoring brings the final sample size to 1,748 individuals, 875 belonging to the control group and 873 belonging to the treatment group.

3.1 Descriptive statistics for the outcomes

This study focuses on three outcomes: unemployment rates, dependency on other public transfers, and earnings. Table 1 shows the means of the three outcome variables. I measure the means of the outcome variables at time -12 (12 months prior to incarceration).

---

[10]This includes all who have been convicted to detainment, since these are categorised as mentally ill.
[11]Women and individuals aged 46 or older at the time of the crime made up 3.7% of the sample at this point.

Data

Table 1: Means of the outcomes variables

Variable	Mean	Std. Dev.
Unemployed	0.33	0.46
Dependent on other public transfers	0.15	0.48
Earnings, 2005 DKK	8,843	11,507
N	1,748	

Source: Based on own calculations using data from Statistics Denmark.

The table shows that the sample had few resources as measured by the three outcomes. Average monthly earnings (gross earnings excluding public transfers) were approximately DKK 8,800[12] (EUR 1,180). Further, sizable proportions of the sample - 33 and 15 percent respectively - were unemployed or dependent on other public transfers at time -12.

Table 2 presents the corresponding means of the outcome variables for the treatment and control groups, along with the p-values for a t-test for differences in the means, in order to investigate whether the reform was unrelated to the two groups' labor market outcomes prior to incarceration.

Table 2: Means of the outcome variables by treatment status

Variable	Control	Treatment	P-value
Unemployed	0.33	0.33	0.94
Dependent on other public transfers	0.15	0.15	0.95
Earnings, 2005 DKK	9,118	8,566	0.32
N	875	873	

Source: Based on own calculations using data from Statistics Denmark.

The table shows no significant differences in any of the outcome variables.

Figure 3 depicts the monthly rates of unemployment for the sample together with the monthly dependency on other public transfers for each of the two groups, from time -60 to time 36.

The figure shows that approximately 20 percent of both the control and the treatment groups were unemployed 60 months prior to incarceration, and that the two fractions followed each other closely thereafter. The rates increased during the last three years prior to incarceration to almost 40 percent, and the unemployment rates for both groups show large increases upon release. Thereafter, the rates for both groups dropped steadily over the remainder of the period, but the drop was greatest for the treatment group. The rates of unemployment for the two groups did not differ significantly from each other in any of the 60 months prior to incarceration.

Furthermore, the figure shows that the average dependency on other public transfers was initially approximately 12 percent for both groups, though slightly higher for the control group. For both groups, dependency on other public transfers increased slightly over the period up until the time of incarceration. After release, dependency on other public transfers

---
[12] In 2005 prices DKK 1 corresponds to EUR 0.134.

Figure 3: Average rates of unemployment and dependency on other public transfers for the control and treatment groups

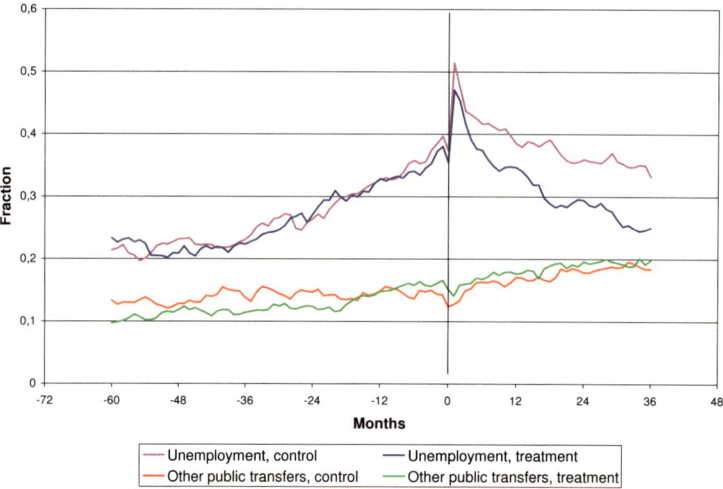

Source: Based on own calculations using data from Statistics Denmark.

for both groups increased evenly toward the end of the depicted period shown, to a level of almost 20 percent. While some of the differences between the treatment and the control groups are significant at a 5 percent level, all differences observed less than 30 months prior to incarceration are insignificant.

Figure 4 shows the average monthly earnings of both groups, from time -60 to time 36.

Figure 4: Average earnings for the control and treatment groups

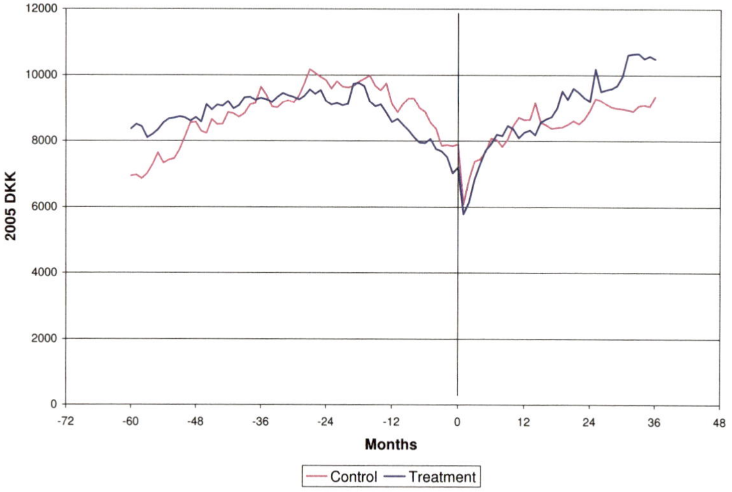

Source: Based on own calculations using data from Statistics Denmark.

As figure 4 shows, monthly earnings were approximately DKK 8,000 (EUR 1,072) for both groups 60 months prior to incarceration. Average earnings of both groups increased over the subsequent three years. However, there was a drop during the last two and a half year prior to incarceration. Upon release, average earnings increased monotonically, though the increase was largest for the treatment group. The average earnings of the two groups were not significantly different from each other at a 5 percent significance level in any of the months during the last four years leading up to the incarceration spell, except in one single month (at time -8).

3.2 Descriptive statistics for the covariates

Table 3 shows summary statistics for the characteristics of the offenders and indicators of previous criminal history. I measure the socio-economic variables presented in the table at time -12, while I measure the indicators of previous criminal history at time 0.

Table 3: Summary staticstics of the sample

Variable	Mean	Std. Dev.
Age	28.13	7.80
Married	0.23	0.42
Cohabitant	0.28	0.45
Have children	0.36	0.48
Non-western immigrants or descendants	0.12	0.48
Employed	0.52	0.48
No job-qualifying education	0.67	0.47
Vocational or skilled	0.23	0.42
Upper secondary or higher	0.10	0.30
Have been convicted before	0.83	0.37
Have been convicted of a violent crime before	0.48	0.50
Have been convicted of a property crime before	0.67	0.47
Months since 1st date of crime leading to an indictment	109	83
Months since 1st date of crime leading to an conviction	98	84
Months since 1st incarceration	46	73
First conviction (if any) was for a violent crime	0.18	0.44
Number of previous convictions	4.44	5.89
N	1,748	

Source: Based on own calculations using data from Statistics Denmark.

The table shows that the sample had a low level of resources as measured by socio-economic variables. Relatively few were employed, the majority had taken no education beyond secondary school and few were married or cohabiting. Table 3 also shows that the offenders on average experienced their first recorded contact with the police at time -109. Further, they had committed their first crime for which they were convicted at time -98, and 18 percent of these crimes were violent. On average, they had experienced their first incarceration at time -46. More than 80 percent had received a conviction prior to the one studied in this paper. 43 percent had been convicted of a violent crime, whereas 64 percent had received convictions for a property crime. Finally, the average individual in the sample had more than four convictions prior to the one in question.

Table 4 shows descriptive statistics for the sample by treatment status, together with the p-values for a t-test of differences between the means of the two groups. Like table 2, this comparison shows whether the reform was the only difference between the two groups.

Table 4: Summary statistics of the sample by treatment status

Variable	Control	Treatment	P-value
Age	28.40	27.86	0.15
Married	0.26	0.20	<0.01
Cohabitant	0.28	0.27	0.65
Have children	0.38	0.34	0.10
Non-western immigrants or descendants	0.11	0.13	0.24
Employed	0.52	0.52	0.97
No job-qualifying education	0.68	0.67	0.73
Vocational or skilled	0.23	0.23	0.71
Upper secondary or higher	0.09	0.10	0.98
Have been convicted before	0.83	0.83	0.98
Have been convicted of a violent crime before	0.50	0.47	0.20
Have been convicted of a property crime before	0.67	0.66	0.49
Months since 1st crime leading to an indictment	110	108	0.64
Months since 1st crime leading to an conviction	99	97	0.53
Months since 1st incar.	47	44	0.51
First conviction (if any) was for violent crime	0.17	0.19	0.44
Number of previous convictions	4.45	4.43	0.94
N	875	873	

Source: Based on own calculations using data from Statistics Denmark.

As the table shows, significantly more of the controls were married and fewer of the treated had children. I find no other significant differences between the two groups.

In addition to individual-level characteristics, I also need to consider potential macro-level differences. Denmark experienced a small recession that began in late 2001 and ended at the beginning of 2004. The recession was followed by a boom that lasted for the remaining part of the data period covered by this paper. However, figures 3 and 4 indicate that the labor market outcomes for the two groups were not affected from these potential differences. In addition, the official policy on the transition from life in prison to life outside did not change during the period of time covered by this paper. Hence, I conclude that the two groups faced the same general conditions on the labor market before and after their incarceration spells, and that there is little sign of any change in the average characteristics of the "violent offender" across the reform, nor any sign of a difference between the two groups as a result of macroeconomic trends. Consequently, the reform therefore provided an exogenous increase in incarceration length, as the two groups also were subject to equal trends in labor market outcomes.

It should be noted that the time paths of both the unemployment rate and earnings display a spike/dip in the months leading up to incarceration. The spikes/dips could indicate the initiation of a criminal trajectory. Additionally, they display a great resemblance to Ashenfelter's dip (Ashenfelter (1978)). As Ashenfelter suggested with regard to the effect evaluation in labor economics, the spikes/dips noted in this paper imply that there might be a large degree of self-selection into incarceration. However, the magnitudes of the spikes/dips do not differ between the treatment and control groups and I can therefore disregard them in the further analysis.

4 Econometric Framework

This paper evaluates the effect of a treatment (i.e. a reform of the Penal Code) on subsequent labor market outcomes. I assess this treatment effect by following the terminology first introduced by Rubin (1974) and adopted by the general treatment literature, and define the treatment effect on the treated as:

$$\delta_{ATT} = E(\delta \mid D_i = 1) = E(y_i(1) \mid D_i = 1) - E(y_i(0) \mid D_i = 1) \qquad (1)$$

where D_i is a binary treatment indicator equal to 1 if i receives treatment and 0 otherwise. $y_i(1)$ denotes the outcome for individual i sentenced under the post-reform guidelines and $y_i(0)$ for the same person sentenced under the pre-reform guidelines. In other words δ_{ATT} expresses the difference between the expected outcomes for individual i in the treatment and control states respectively, under the condition that he is eligible for treatment. Obviously I cannot in reality observe individual i in both states. However, if the treatment is completely random I may substitute $E(y_i(0) \mid D_i = 1)$ with $E(y_i(0) \mid D_i = 0)$, as these are equal. In order to reduce the variance of the estimated effect, it is convenient to condition on independent covariates. Given the exogeneity of the reform, $E(y_i(0) \mid x_i, D_i = 1) = E(y_i(0) \mid x_i, D_i = 0)$ is also satisfied. Following Rosenbaum and Rubin (1983) I may therefore alternatively obtain δ_{ATT} as:

$$\delta_{ATT} = E(\delta \mid D_i = 1) = E(y_i(1) \mid x_i, D_i = 1) - E(y_i(0) \mid x_i, D_i = 0) \qquad (2)$$

Imposing a parametric form to the relationship between the outcome y, the observable characteristics x, the reform D and the unobserved components over time (defined as months), I may express this as:

$$y_{is} = \beta x_{is} + \delta D_i + a_i + e_{is} \qquad (3)$$

where y_{is} is a given labor market outcome for individual i in month $s > 0$ (that is, month s after the incarceration at time 0), x_{is} is a set of observable characteristics summarizing human capital, etc. that account for observed differences between individuals, a is an unobserved fixed effect and e is an unobserved idiosyncratic error term. δ is the parameter of interest - i.e. the effect on y of the increase in incarceration length induced by the reform.

Keeping in mind that D_i is a dummy indicator of the treatment that I seek to evaluate over several periods from time of release s - while correcting for pre-incarceration levels and personal characteristics - I obtain:

$$\Delta y_{is} = \beta \Delta x_{is} + \sum_{s=2}^{s=36} \gamma_s ds + \sum_{s=1}^{s=36} \delta_s D_i + \Delta e_{is} \qquad (4)$$

by differencing of equation (3) with time -12 (that is, 12 months prior to the beginning of the incarceration spell). Hence $\Delta y_{is} = y_{is} - y_{i,-12}$, $\Delta x_{is} = x_{is} - x_{i,-12}$, $\Delta e_{is} = e_{is} - e_{i,-12}$, β is a vector measuring the effects of the covariates,[13] and d_s is an indicator of time since release equal to 1 if $time = s$ and 0 otherwise. δ_s is the effect of the reform on the labor market outcomes in period s. Thus δ_s captures the effect of the reform in each month since release, for a total of three years.

In order to obtain consistent results, none of the terms I include in equation (4) may correlate with the unobserved components. Section 3 showed that neither the magnitude of the dip nor the trends and levels of the outcome variables prior to incarceration differed significantly across the two groups, and the reform provided an exogenous shift in incarceration length (so D_i is orthogonal to the unobserved factors embedded in the time invariant a_i and the idiosyncratic error e_{is}). In addition, the conditions apply to the covariates. The econometric framework therefore applies a method that eliminates all time-invariant variables, including a_i, because the condition that personal characteristics $E(a_i x_{is}) = 0$ is likely not satisfied.

If prior and recent levels of characteristics x are independent of the idiosyncratic error term e, if the reform provides an exogenous shift in incarceration length, and if the parameters β and δ_s from equation (4) are homogeneous across individuals, I can estimate the parameters consistently by OLS. As the observable differences between the two groups are negligible, it seems reasonable to assume that there are no fundamental differences between the unobserved characteristics of the two groups. Thus I consider the conditions to be satisfied.

5 Results

I measure unemployment rates and dependency on other public transfers in percentages. Hence, a parameter estimate of e.g. 0.01 corresponds to an increase in the respective rate of 1 percentage point. I measure earnings on a monthly basis, hence the parameter estimate corresponds to a change in earnings in DKK (2005 prices: DKK 1 = EUR 0.13) per month.[14] Earnings are by definition zero for persons who are unemployed. Note that the estimates (δ's) are not cumulative; i.e. a parameter estimate of 0.01 one year after release implies that individuals from the treatment group experienced an outcome one percentage point higher than the control group, all else equal, at that given time - regardless of the sign and size of the earlier estimates.

5.1 Main estimation results

Table 5 shows the results of (δ_s) from month 1 to month 36 after release - i.e., the effect of incarceration length identified by the reform on the three outcome variables - together with the standard errors of the estimates in parentheses.[15]

---

[13] Δx includes a constant term, changes in four agesplines, changes in marital status, changes in children, three indicators of changes in education status and changes in area of residence.

[14] Though it is customary, I do not use log earnings because 77 percent of the sample experience months with zero earnings.

[15] As proposed by Bertrand, Duflo, and Mullainathan (2004), DID estimations of treatment effects tend to overrate the significance of the given treatment, because ordinary standard errors fail to take account of

Results

Table 5: Estimation results

Months	Unemployment		Public transfers		Earnings	
1	-0.052**	(0.025)	0.014	(0.018)	334	(493)
2	-0.031	(0.026)	0.029	(0.020)	-196	(541)
3	-0.029	(0.026)	0.015	(0.020)	-40	(524)
4	-0.048*	(0.025)	0.012	(0.019)	361	(525)
5	-0.054**	(0.026)	0.013	(0.021)	434	(556)
6	-0.045*	(0.026)	0.008	(0.021)	207	(575)
7	-0.062**	(0.026)	0.012	(0.021)	695	(672)
8	-0.066***	(0.026)	0.018	(0.020)	765	(566)
9	-0.067***	(0.026)	0.011	(0.020)	893	(669)
10	-0.066***	(0.026)	0.020	(0.020)	489	(572)
11	-0.056***	(0.026)	0.015	(0.020)	-55	(590)
12	-0.045***	(0.027)	0.000	(0.020)	238	(569)
13	-0.048***	(0.026)	0.003	(0.020)	317	(576)
14	-0.067***	(0.026)	0.012	(0.020)	-256	(834)
15	-0.076***	(0.026)	0.012	(0.021)	633	(583)
16	-0.070***	(0.026)	-0.001	(0.020)	728	(571)
17	-0.096***	(0.026)	0.024	(0.021)	421	(576)
18	-0.105***	(0.026)	0.032	(0.022)	573	(591)
19	-0.098***	(0.026)	0.028	(0.022)	1,260**	(635)
20	-0.082***	(0.026)	0.014	(0.022)	926	(610)
21	-0.076***	(0.026)	0.006	(0.021)	1,321**	(603)
22	-0.067***	(0.026)	0.008	(0.021)	1,093*	(597)
23	-0.066***	(0.026)	0.009	(0.021)	1,020*	(600)
24	-0.071***	(0.026)	0.019	(0.021)	722	(594)
25	-0.080***	(0.026)	0.018	(0.021)	1,372*	(735)
26	-0.082***	(0.026)	0.017	(0.021)	653	(610)
27	-0.072***	(0.026)	0.017	(0.022)	718	(633)
28	-0.088***	(0.026)	0.021	(0.021)	933	(643)
29	-0.100***	(0.026)	0.017	(0.021)	973	(644)
30	-0.096***	(0.026)	0.017	(0.021)	1,184*	(622)
31	-0.105***	(0.025)	0.013	(0.021)	1,933***	(664)
32	-0.097***	(0.025)	-0.001	(0.021)	1,985***	(643)
33	-0.102***	(0.025)	-0.002	(0.022)	1,891***	(637)
34	-0.112***	(0.025)	0.014	(0.021)	1,819***	(610)
35	-0.112***	(0.026)	0.010	(0.021)	1,980***	(602)
36	-0.091***	(0.025)	0.013	(0.021)	1,499***	(608)
R^2	0.030		0.016		0.030	
N	1,748					

Significance levels: * : 10% ** : 5% *** : 1%

Unemployment   The table shows that all of the estimates are negative and, except for six of the estimates within the first year after release, significant at a 5 percent significance level. The sizes of the estimates indicate that the reform induced a drop in the unemployment rate of approximately 4 to 5 percentage points. As time since release increases, so does the numerical size of the estimates, to a level of roughly 7 to 10 percentage points two years after release. This level is persistent for the remaining estimates. Thus, the reform has resulted in significantly lower unemployment rates, and the effect increases with time since release.

Dependency on other public transfers   The table shows that all of the estimates (apart from two) are positive. Nonetheless, they are all numerically small, and insignificant even at a ten percent level. The estimates are neither significant when tested jointly. One might have suspected that there was a substitution between unemployment and other public transfers. However, the insignificant estimates of dependency on other public transfers reject this hypothesis.[16] This finding thus suggests that the change in incarceration length which followed the reform increased employment for the sample.

Earnings   The estimated effects on earnings exhibit greater volatility than the estimates with unemployment and dependency on public transfers. In addition, the estimates show no effect of the reform on subsequent earnings during the first 18 months after release. After the first 18 months the estimates show a positive and significant effect of the reform of approximately DKK 1,000 (EUR 134) per month. This effect is persistent and even slightly increasing over time, to around DKK 1,500 (EUR 201) more per month three years after release. The estimates thus suggest a positive effect from the increase in incarceration length, as induced by the reform, and that this effect increases over time. The data do not allow me to determine whether the earnings increases appear due to higher levels of productivity or lower levels of unemployment. However, since table 5 also shows that employment increased for the treated, resulting in a greater number of individuals with none-zero earnings, I suspect this to be the dominant factor.

---

serial correlation in the outcomes which is often observed in outcomes related to the labor market. They emphasise that even the "normal" heteroskedastic-robust standard errors does not correct the bias. As one solution, they propose to obtain the standard errors of the estimates by a wild-bootstrapping procedure.

This paper applies a wild-bootstrap procedure as proposed by Flachaire (2005); Davidson and Flachaire (2008), with $\rho_{is} = \begin{cases} -1 \text{ with probability } 0.5 \\ 1 \text{ with probability } 0.5 \end{cases}$, so $E(\rho_{is}) = 0$ and $\sigma_\rho^2 = 1$.

[16]In order to investigate the possibility of opposing effects within the composite measure of dependency on other public transfers, I have estimated the model with a subdivision of this outcome into two general categories: first, voluntary efforts revealing an interest in (re-)entering the labor market at some point, e.g. financial support for education, financial aid for upgrading work-oriented skills, specific voluntary labor market programs; and second, mandatory programs required in order to be eligible for the receipt of benefits or passive support without any requirements, such as sick leave, early retirement relating to lack of employablity, etc. Common to all the types of benefits included in the second group is that they are not aimed at obtaining employment on the labor market in the future. The first group of outcomes were unaffected by the reform, while there was a weak sign of an increase in the second category as a consequence of the reform. However, this result was neither sufficiently robust nor significant on a sufficient level for any conclusions to be drawn.

Additionally, I have estimated the model with total dependency on public transfers (the sum of unemployment and dependency on other public transfers). The results using this outcome did not change any conclusions, as they were not significantly different from those with rate of unemployment as an outcome. Hence, I conclude that the results are not caused by a substitution effect.

5.2 Macroeconomic trends

Identifying an effect using a reform may pose a problem if the reform is introduced parallel to other macro-level changes. In such a case the pre- and post-reform groups would be subject to other macroeconomic trends, which I would - wrongfully - ascribe as being effects of reform. To investigate whether this is a problem in my analysis, I restrict the sample such that I only include persons sentenced to imprisonment for a crime committed 6 months prior to or after the implementation of the reform (rather than 18 months), reducing the sample size to 611 - 361 in the control group and 250 in the treatment group. The reduced sample size may affect significance levels. However, it should not affect the size of the estimates from table 5, if these are robust.

Table 6 shows the estimates (corresponding to table 5), together with the standard errors of the estimates in parentheses.[17]

The table reveals some noteworthy differences between the original estimates from table 5 and those obtained using the restricted sample, both in size and level of significance. First, the estimated parameters of the effect on the unemployment rate for the first 18 months are generally numerically larger than the estimates presented in table 5 and the majority are highly significant. Second, the estimated effects on dependency on other public transfers show some sign of a positive effect from the reform. However, the estimates are only significant for the first year since release and additionally, the size and significance of the estimates are not consistent, as the estimates from the full time-span sample are numerically smaller than those obtained with the refined sample.[18] Third, the estimated effects on earnings from table 6 display some differences when compared with those obtained from the full time-span sample. Hence, there is little evidence of the positive effect on earnings found in the initial estimates. The coefficients are of mixed sign and only one is significant at a 5 percent level.

In general, I expected fewer estimates to be significantly different from zero, due to the heavily reduced sample size. I must nevertheless accept the change of sign of some coefficients as being an indicator lack of robustness. Hence, it is possible that the positive effect on earnings obtained in the first model results from different macroeconomic settings rather than from the reform. In contrast, the effect on unemployment rates appears robust, as it shifted in the opposite direction of the probable macro-trend bias. To confirm this, I define a series of pseudo-reforms for each month from July 1999 to June 2005 and test for joint significance for the effects on unemployment. The pseudo-reforms that do not coincide with the time of the reform at June 2002 should all be insignificant, while the effects for the time around the real reform should be significant. Figure 5 shows the p-value for a Wald-test for joint significance.[19]

---

[17] Again, I have calculated the standard errors using a wild-bootstrap procedure.

[18] Again, I have estimated the model using total dependency on public transfers. The results were not significantly different from those for unemployment. Therefore, they suggest that the rate of unemployment dropped as a consequence of the reform, while there was no attrition from the labor market, as the reform did not affect dependency on other public transfers.

[19] For each pseudo-reform, the data are constructed as described in Section 3. Hence, each new sample includes violent crimes committed in a period of 18 months on each side of the pseudo-reform.

Table 6: Estimation results reduced time span

Months	Unemployment		Public transfers		Earnings	
1	-0.090**	(0.042)	0.067**	(0.028)	-150	(812)
2	-0.058	(0.043)	0.089***	(0.032)	-901	(836)
3	-0.064	(0.042)	0.090***	(0.034)	-710	(879)
4	-0.064	(0.042)	0.069**	(0.035)	-224	(912)
5	-0.082**	(0.041)	0.074***	(0.035)	-194	(977)
6	-0.074*	(0.041)	0.065**	(0.033)	-264	(1,049)
7	-0.113***	(0.041)	0.083***	(0.034)	241	(954)
8	-0.103***	(0.041)	0.064*	(0.034)	732	(955)
9	-0.121***	(0.042)	0.062*	(0.034)	1,188	(914)
10	-0.141***	(0.042)	0.070**	(0.033)	782	(932)
11	-0.154***	(0.042)	0.079**	(0.033)	427	(912)
12	-0.130***	(0.043)	0.069**	(0.035)	23	(942)
13	-0.143***	(0.042)	0.070**	(0.034)	564	(941)
14	-0.168***	(0.042)	0.084**	(0.034)	737	(956)
15	-0.192***	(0.043)	0.076**	(0.035)	1,536	(986)
16	-0.163***	(0.044)	0.032	(0.035)	1,936**	(945)
17	-0.164***	(0.044)	0.046	(0.035)	1,667	(978)
18	-0.144***	(0.044)	0.052	(0.035)	1,344	(966)
19	-0.147***	(0.043)	0.060*	(0.035)	2,222*	(1,187)
20	-0.107**	(0.045)	0.044	(0.037)	878	(952)
21	-0.116***	(0.043)	0.042	(0.037)	1,050	(963)
22	-0.101**	(0.044)	0.030	(0.037)	1,172	(977)
23	-0.105**	(0.043)	0.046	(0.037)	611	(976)
24	-0.104**	(0.044)	0.066*	(0.038)	-300	(1,002)
25	-0.142***	(0.044)	0.076**	(0.039)	1,201	(1,506)
26	-0.113***	(0.045)	0.072*	(0.038)	-786	(1,111)
27	-0.106**	(0.044)	0.078**	(0.037)	531	(1,053)
28	-0.086**	(0.044)	0.071*	(0.038)	-1,108	(1,092)
29	-0.085**	(0.044)	0.057	(0.037)	-1,534	(1,260)
30	-0.106**	(0.044)	0.052	(0.036)	-253	(1,037)
31	-0.124***	(0.043)	0.057	(0.037)	829	(1,188)
32	-0.080*	(0.043)	0.038	(0.037)	690	(1,067)
33	-0.104**	(0.045)	0.040	(0.036)	983	(1,063)
34	-0.107**	(0.045)	0.063*	(0.037)	381	(1,034)
35	-0.105**	(0.044)	0.051	(0.037)	240	(1,036)
36	-0.107***	(0.043)	0.054	(0.036)	-196	(990)
R^2	0.052		0.052		0.039	
N	611					

Significance levels: * : 10%   ** : 5%   *** : 1%

Figure 5: Significance level for joint tests of pseudo reforms on unemployment rate

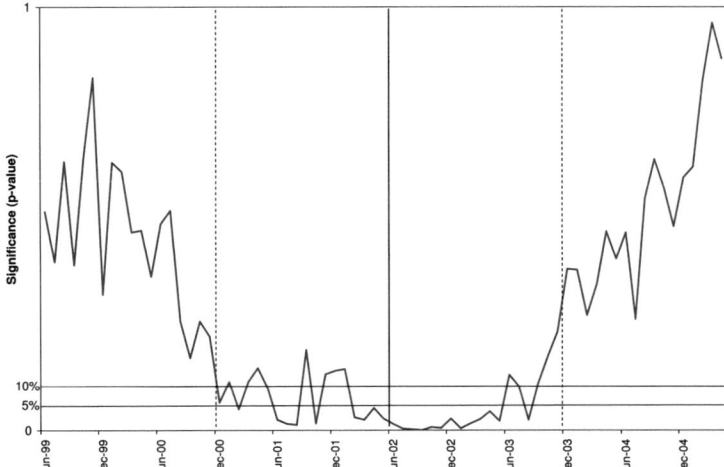

The vertical solid line marks the time of the reform. The vertical dotted lines mark a time-span from 18 months prior to the reform and 18 months after the reform, to indicate where the associated time-span coincide with the real reform.

The figure shows that the effects of every pseudo-reform applied to data that do not include June 2002 are insignificant. As the pseudo-reforms approaches the timing of the real reform, the levels of significance increase. This confirms that the effects of the reform are robust and not caused by macroeconomic trends or fluctuations.

5.3 Non-zero earnings

By definition, monthly earnings are zero if an individual experiences full unemployment in a given month. 459 individuals from the full time-span sample and 151 from the restricted sample were unemployed for all the 36 months after release. In the following, I restrict the sample to the fractions of the full time-span and restricted time-span-samples who obtained employment in at least one of the first 36 months after release from incarceration. Table 7 shows the estimates with earnings as outcome.

When the first set of estimates in table 7 are compared to the last two columns in table 5, no noteworthy differences are found. The size, signs and levels of significance are approximately alike. However, when the second set of estimates in table 7 are compared to those in table 6, we see that eliminating fully-unemployed individuals results in an increased number of significant positive estimates. Further, the effects of the reform on the earnings of the individuals who actually obtained employment are jointly significant. Hence, the table show a positive effect on earnings from the increase in incarceration length for those who were in employment.

Table 7: Estimation results with non-zero earnings

	Full time-span				Restricted time-span			
Months	Earnings	Months	Earnings	Months	Earnings	Months	Earnings
1	594	(628)	19	1,648**	(846)	1	-5	(1,138)	19	3,170**	(1,548)
2	-137	(686)	20	1,196	(818)	2	-1,006	(1,219)	20	1,588	(1,255)
3	55	(672)	21	1,764**	(797)	3	-1,020	(1,145)	21	1,881	(1,284)
4	559	(657)	22	1,432*	(779)	4	-363	(1,144)	22	2,052*	(1,235)
5	607	(720)	23	1,312*	(770)	5	-198	(1,210)	23	1,256	(1,226)
6	309	(750)	24	936	(783)	6	-124	(1,383)	24	69	(1,249)
7	945	(743)	25	1,781*	(952)	7	1,165	(1,297)	25	1,932	(1,854)
8	1050	(748)	26	853	(814)	8	1,766	(1,323)	26	-638	(1,413)
9	1235	(720)	27	95	(826)	9	2,167	(1,247)	27	-418	(1,354)
10	654	(736)	28	1,218	(824)	10	1,634	(1,249)	28	-1,183	(1,409)
11	-95	(787)	29	1,247	(856)	11	1,133	(1,216)	29	1,701	(1,588)
12	326	(766)	30	1,536*	(813)	12	427	(1,215)	30	-142	(1,348)
13	448	(757)	31	2,505***	(851)	13	958	(1,247)	31	1,391	(1,564)
14	-311	(1,085)	32	2,581***	(843)	14	1,654	(1,240)	32	1,375	(1,365)
15	912	(760)	33	2,484***	(815)	15	2,554**	(1,228)	33	1,841	(1,340)
16	1,005	(758)	34	2,357***	(797)	16	3,026***	(1,180)	34	986	(1,315)
17	557	(791)	35	2,554***	(791)	17	2,048	(1,298)	35	742	(1,313)
18	767	(776)	36	1,931***	(826)	18	1,352	(1,387)	36	272	(1,242)
R^2	0.035					0.044			
N	1,289					460			

Significance levels: * : 10%   ** : 5%   *** : 1%

6 Conclusion

This paper investigates how incarceration length affects unemployment rates, dependency on other public transfers and earnings. I use a reform of the Danish Penal Code in 2002 to facilitate causal inference.

My estimates showed that an increase in incarceration length resulted in persistently lower rates of unemployment in a sample of violent offenders. During the first year after release, unemployment rates were 4 to 5 percentage points lower than for those who committed crime prior to the reform, and the difference increased in subsequent years. These results were robust with respect to limitation of the time-span and also to a series of pseudo-reforms. In contrast, dependency on other public transfers was not affected by the reform. This suggests that the increase in incarceration length increased the residual outcome *employment*. Finally, the effects on earnings continued to increase with time after release. However, the increases in earnings were not robust with respect to limitation in the time-span. Nevertheless, the fraction of the treatment group who found employment experienced a positive significant effect on earnings; even when the time-span was limited. I therefore conclude that the increase in incarceration length, resulted in higher earnings for the employed.

6.1 Limitation and discussion

The conclusion that longer incarceration length does not result in worse, but possibly better labor market outcomes is in accordance with the results from Needles (1996) and Kling (2006). It seems unreasonable to assume that the results stem from changes in human capital, as the reform only increased the average incarceration lengths by approximately 7 days. Instead, the results suggest that the increase in incarceration length as a result of the reform actually increased participation in rehabilitating programs in prison for which an offender's pre-reform sentence would have been too short, otherwise leaving the offenders solely with the possible stigma, job-loss and general alienation from the labor market which incarceration might involve. This proposition is in accordance with a report by Flemming Balvig, Professor in Criminal Law, produced in cooperation with The Danish Bar and Law Society (Balvig (2006)). Balvig describes the chances of entering rehabilitation during a short incarceration spell in a Danish prison as follows:

"Convicted offenders who are sentenced to the shortest incarceration spells are in practice only able to use the prisons' rehabilitating services to a very limited degree (...) Prisons do not draft plans of action for the time of incarceration and for the release of the offenders, as a consequence of the short incarceration spells." [Balvig (2006, pp. 12), own translation].

Hence, the longer incarceration spells induced by the reform may have increased labor market outcomes simply by giving prison authorities additional time to aid the offender at the time of release. Intuitively, the lower costs of job-search and higher social capital should increase employment and earnings, as long as they outweigh the stigma from the increased incarceration length - which the results suggest is the case.

Moreover, the sizes of the estimates on unemployment rates and earnings also suggest a positive long-run effect of the reform using a back-of-an-envelope cost-benefit calculation. I derive this by using the estimated effects on unemployment and earnings to proxy savings on social assistance and increased tax revenue while correcting for the average costs per offender of the increased incarceration length induced by the reform.[20] The approximation yields a positive net present value within the first 30 months after release, and increases for subsequent months.

The data do not allow me to identify the causes of the effect on earnings, though I suspect the higher level of employment to be the dominant factor. Additionally, the effects may suffer from a selection bias from employment, e.g. as proposed by Needles (1996). Consequently, I cannot extrapolate the positive effect on earnings to the entire sample, but only to those who actually obtained employment.

The results of this paper rely on the exogeneity of the reform. I should therefore consider the possibility that the reform caused the average offender to change. It is reasonable to assume that longer sentences would result in a treatment group that has weaker socio-economic potential than the control group - or in other words, a group with less employment-security and poorer affiliation to the labor market, etc. However, the results (especially for the rate of unemployment) suggest the opposite. The likely direction of bias, if the use of the reform in this setting is endogenous, is thus *not* towards zero. The direction of the bias will be changed indeterminately if the two groups experienced different trends in the outcomes or alternatively if the dips/spikes prior to incarceration differed. The paper shows that this was not the case. Nevertheless, the pre-incarceration dips/spikes call for further study, which should elucidate whether these are a general phenomenon for all offender types and further, how they are related to the criminal acts themselves and the severity of the crimes, in order to uncover any self-selection.

While this paper is very selective with respect to the composition of the sample, there remains noteworthy heterogeneity, which may have obscured the results. Most disturbing are the long tails of the distributions of lengths of incarceration spells. Discarding the observations from the tails could provide a more homogeneous sample. However, selecting observations on grounds of incarceration length would reintroduce the endogeneity that the paper has attempted to avoid. In addition, if the increase in incarceration lengths from the reform was local and not general, the results are a local average treatment effect rather average treatment effect on the treated. It may be that the results are arise because some proportion of the sample received e.g. a sentence of two instead of one month of incarceration. Yet, this does not change the general interpretation of the results.

The conclusion is only valid for the subgroup of violent offenders that made up the sample and it is not a general treatment effect that can be extrapolated to cover other offender types. However, if the origin of the positive effects of these changes in incarceration length on employment and earnings resulted from increased programme participation, the conclusions may hold for other types of offenders who receive sentences of around a one or two months. Hence, an obvious task for future analysis is to test the conclusion on other offender types. It is also worthwhile considering whether very short sentences only serve to stigmatize offenders without providing any proper rehabilitation or aid with the transition to life at liberty. E.g. policy-makers and judges may consider whether very short sentences of imprisonment could usefully be replaced by suspended sentences or community service, without violating the victims' sense of justice. And where imprisonment is deemed necessary, the various

---

[20] The average cost of one week of incarceration in 2002 was approximately DKK 8,763 (EUR 1,174) in 2005 prices, according to the Danish Prison and Probation Service.

stakeholders should perhaps consider the offender's possibilities of rehabilitation to a greater degree.

References

ALMLUND, M., A. L. DUCKWORTH, J. J. HECKMAN, AND T. D. KAUTZ (2011): "Personality psychology and economics," Discussion Paper 16822, National Bureau of Economic Research.

ASHENFELTER, O. (1978): "Estimating the Effect of Training Programs on Earnings," *The Review of Economics and Statistics*, 60(1), 47–57.

BALVIG, F. (2006): "Ni anbefalinger fra arbejdsgruppen om fremtidens straffe," Discussion paper, Advokatsamfundet.

BECKER, G. S. (1994): *Human Capital: A Theoretical and Empirical Analysis, with Special Reference to Education*. University Of Chicago Press, 3 edn.

BERTRAND, M., E. DUFLO, AND S. MULLAINATHAN (2004): "How Much Should We Trust Differences-in-Differences Estimates?," *Quarterly Journal of Economics*, 119(1), 249–275.

CUNHA, F., AND J. HECKMAN (2008): "Formulating, identifying and estimating the technology of cognitive and noncognitive skill formation," *Journal of Human Resources*, 43(4), 738–782.

CUNHA, F., J. HECKMAN, AND S. SCHENNACH (2010): "Estimating the technology of cognitive and noncognitive skill formation," *Econometrica*, 78(3), 883–931.

DAVIDSON, R., AND E. FLACHAIRE (2008): "The wild bootstrap, tamed at last," *Journal of Econometrics*, 146(1), 162–169.

FLACHAIRE, E. (2005): "Bootstrapping heteroskedastic regression models: wild bootstrap vs. pairs bootstrap," *Computational Statistics & Data Analysis*, 49(2), 361–376.

FREEMAN, R. B. (1992): "Crime and the Employment of Disadvantaged Youths," in *Urban Labor Markets and Job Opportunities*, ed. by G. Peterson, and W. Vroman. The Urban Institutes Press, Washington D.C.

GLAESER, E., D. LAIBSON, AND B. SACERDOTE (2002): "An Economic Approach to Social Capital.," *Economic Journal*, 112(483), 437–458.

GRANOVETTER, M. S. (1995): *Getting a job*. University of Chicago Press, Chicago, (IL), 2 edn.

GROGGER, J. (1995): "The Effect of Arrests on the Employment and Earnings of Young Men," *The Quarterly Journal of Economics*, 110(1), 51–71.

HOLZER, H. J. (1988): "Search Method Use by Unemployed Youth," *Journal of Labor Economics*, 6(1), 1–20.

JENCKS, C. (1972): *Inequality: A Reassessment of the Effect of Family and Schooling in America*. Basic Books, 2nd printing edn.

KLING, J. R. (2006): "Incarceration Length, Employment, and Earnings," *American Economic Review*, 96(3), 863–876.

References

Landersø, R., and T. Tranæs (2009): "Selvforsørgelse og uddannelse efter fængsel," in *Løsladt - og hvad så?*, ed. by Rybjerg, vol. 2009, pp. 189–211. Jurist- og økonomforbundets Forlag, Copenhagen, DK, 1 edn.

Lott, J. R. (1992a): "An Attempt at Measuring the Total Monetary Penalty from Drug Convictions: The Importance of an Individual's Reputation," *The Journal of Legal Studies*, 21(1), 159–187.

Lott, J. R. (1992b): "Do We Punish High Income Criminals Too Heavily?," *Economic Inquiry*, 30(4), 583–608.

Mincer, J. (1974): *Schooling, Experience, and Earnings. Human Behavior & Social Institutions No. 2*. National Bureau of Economic Research, Inc, New York, NY.

Nagin, D., and J. Waldfogel (1995): "The effects of criminality and conviction on the labor market status of young British offenders," *International Review of Law and Economics*, 15(1), 109–126.

——— (1998): "The Effect of Conviction on Income Through the Life Cycle," *International Review of Law and Economics*, 18(1), 25–40.

Needles, K. S. (1996): "Go directly to jail and do not collect? A long-term study of recidivism, employment, and earnings patterns among prison releases," *Unpublished doctoral dissertation, Princeton University, Department of Economics*, pp. 471–496.

Rosenbaum, P. R., and D. B. Rubin (1983): "The Central Role of the Propensity Score in Observational Studies for Causal Effects," *Biometrika*, 70(1), 41–55.

Rubin, D. B. (1974): "Estimating causal effects of treatments in randomized and nonrandomized studies.," *Journal of Educational Psychology*, 66(5), 688–701.

Sampson, R. J., and J. H. Laub (1995): *Crime in the making: pathways and turning points through life*. Harvard University Press.

Secretary of Justice Lene Espersen (2002): "Betænkning til 2001/2 LF 118," https://www.retsinformation.dk/Forms/R0710.aspx?id=101010.

Tranæs, T. (2008): "Den uformelle straf og velfærdsstaten," *Nordisk Tidsskrift for Kriminalvidenskab*, 95(3), 225–242.

Waldfogel, J. (1994): "The Effect of Criminal Conviction on Income and the Trust "Reposed in the Workmen"," *The Journal of Human Resources*, 29(1), 62–81.

Western, B., J. R. Kling, and D. F. Weiman (2001): "The Labor Market Consequences of Incarceration," *Crime Delinquency*, 47(3), 410–427.